The House Édouard Built,

a Unité at Briey

By Patrick Weber
Edited by Erika Lanselle

First edition, published by East Winter® Books
an imprint of Thought and Company Ltd,
33 London N7 0HU
www.eastwinter.com

While every effort has been made to check the accuracy and quality of the information given in this publication, neither the Author nor the Publisher accept any responsibility for the subsequent use of this information, for any errors or omissions that it may contain, or for any misunderstandings arising from it. However, as this text is a work in progress, please send corrections to: studio@eastwinter.com where every effort will be made to make amendments in a subsequent edition.

Book design and production by East Winter® Books.
Set in IBM Plex.

Some names and identifying details have been changed to protect the privacy of individuals.

ISBN: 978-0-9935046-3-1

Acknowledgments

This book represents a long journey to rediscover and learn to appreciate one of Le Corbusier's Unité's, the one that is usually not part of the architectural canon. For years it was only a sign on a motorway we drove on our way from the UK to Germany and when we first approached it, we didn't fully appreciate the complexities this Unité stands for.

We didn't go on our journey alone, we would like to express our thanks to the residents of Briey who opened their apartments and let us share how they made a home in this iconic building. Especially Beate Heigel, Karole Krezierski and of course the late Pascal Schoening in particular for all the long conversations, the stories of the beginning in the 1990's, squatting with the then unknown painter Peter Doig in the almost abandoned building.

Over time our research was supported from Veronique Leonard representing the Association La Premiere Rue, Briey, with some additional support from Delphine Studer from the Fondation Le Corbusier, Paris without whom this work would not have been as interesting and insightful.

Finally but foremost sound judgement and no little skill has been exercised by Erika Lanselle through her editorial consideration and general guidance.

Patrick Weber
London, July 2020

Introduction

a

3

d

6

e

7

b

4

c

5

f

8

g

9

Images:

pages 3:

a.   The Unité in context, 2019. Located on top of a hill above the town of Briey, the Unité is a concentrated development surrounded by a green landscape.

pages 4–9:

b.   Front elevation.

c.   Le Corbusier's Modular, uniquely amongst Unités this variant features a distinctly geometric reimagining.

d.   The reflected coloured light of the facade soffits.

e.   An in-situ cast stair.

f.   The Briey Unité angular variant of the structural pilotti.

g.   Entrance foyer reception area.

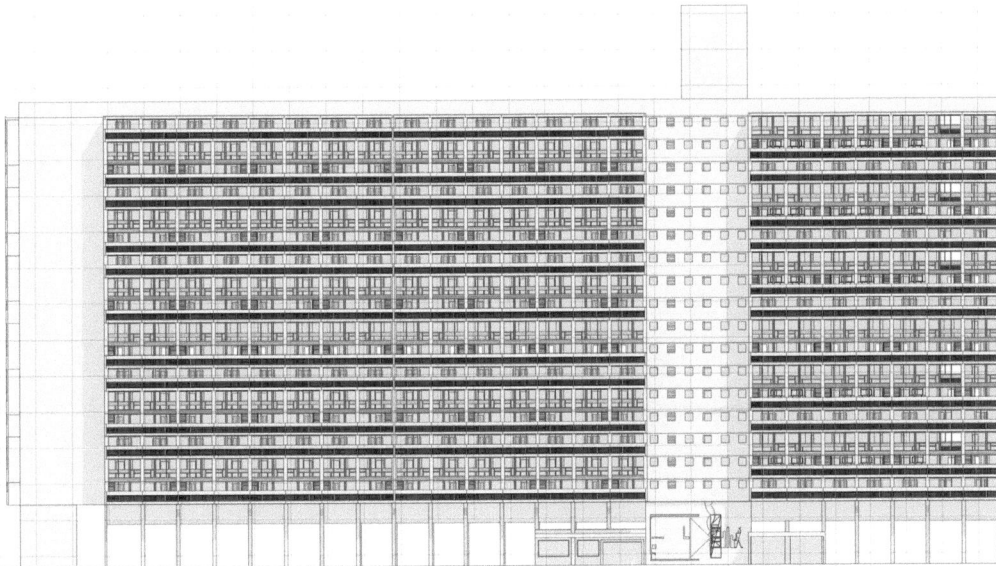

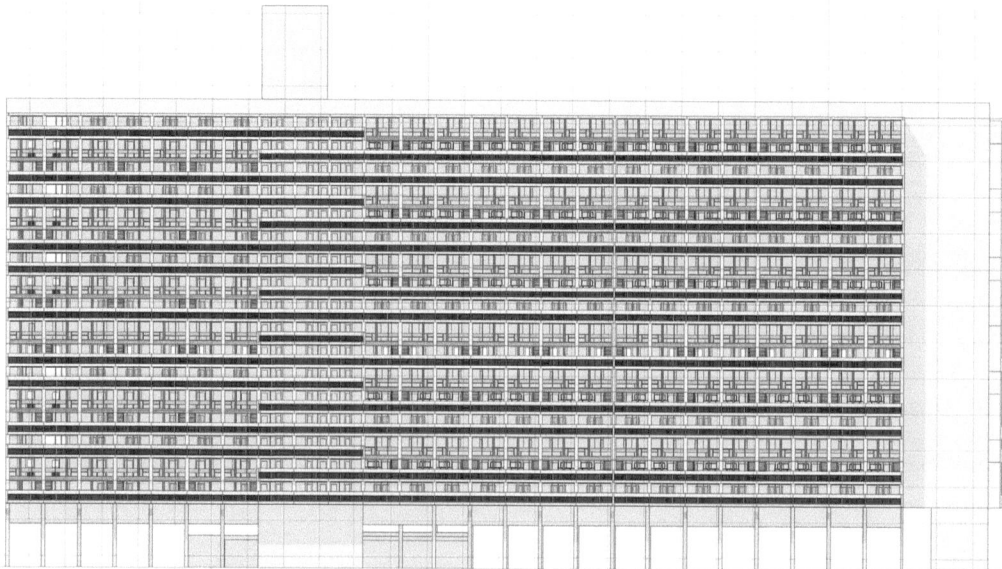

Introduction

This study takes a look at the Unité d'Habitation at Briey-en-Forêt in France (henceforth referred to as Briey), the lesser-known Unité in the canon of Le Corbusier's work, delving into its history whilst addressing parts of the post-design adaptation by various residents.

In light of its complex post-occupancy history, the study adopts qualitative strategies to critically evaluate the idea of architectural success in light of this often overlooked yet significant Le Corbusier project. Of the five Unité housing projects designed by Le Corbusier (1885–1965) f.k.a Charles-Édouard Jeanneret, Briey's Unité was the fourth completed. Its story and situation are considered here to be the most interesting, and possibly the most relevant for many of today's questions on the concerns of housing and mass home building.

Although dismissed by many as a failed project, the present degree of adaptation and sense of community observed over the duration of this study has led to a reconsideration of the criteria for 'success'. Future consideration of adaptability in architecture, of existing frameworks and proposals, could be beneficial to the housing concerns of today.

As such, through a combination of documentary and field based methods this study hopes to engage with the following questions:

1. How well have Le Corbusier's theoretical constructs for living weathered? Does Briey still 'feel' like a LeCorbusier project, with regard to the existing building fabric, its tectonic aspirations, interior design components, and the consequences of change?
2. How do we create a sense of home where a mode of living has been prescribed?
3. How do we define architectural success in the context of changing programmes and occupant alterations? Recognising the lines between an artist's intentions, and a user's desires and aspirations; in the contexts of social-cultural changes.

Built in 1961, the Unité d'Habitation de Briey stands today alongside the Unité in Berlin as one of Le Corbusier's few intended social housing projects, based on a largely self-contained mixed programme format realised more completely through the four other Unités. Designed in accordance to his principles of how modern dwellings and, to an extent, the city should operate, this project was unfortunately not realised to the same construction standards or mixed programme as its four other more valued Unité siblings.

Furthermore, over the years, social and economic decline led to periods of its abandonment and reoccupation as a squat, its recognition as an architectural artistic work (in keeping with the portfolio of Le Corbusier) was overlooked as much of its fitted interior furnishing was stripped out and sold or consumed as firewood. Just as for the other Unité projects, Briey was designed to include many of the programmatic services one might associate with a functioning village: a nursery, shops, restaurants, a hotel, a laundry, to name a few. However, from the outset due in part to its social housing status, last-minute cost cuts, and political maneuvers, these services were never realised, resulting in a reasonably remotely positioned building solely formed of housing.

In 1963, not long after construction, a decline in the region's economy, causing the closure of Briey's mines, saw the project and its community experience financial difficulties until eventually, by 1982 it was mostly abandoned. Since then it was briefly squatted, partially raided, narrowly escaped demolition, before being sold for 1 Franc to the Hospital and partially adapted as a nursing school, with the remainder renovated as affordable housing, and then partially listed as a heritage site to save it from demolition. It has been said, at one point, by residents wishing to remain anonymous, that *'apartment interior stairs were removed and sold for more than the sale values of the apartments'* thus enabled some of the new residents to pay-off their loans. Today it is largely occupied by a relatively diverse community, with varying attitudes towards its consideration as an original 'Le Corbusier' work of architecture—and all that might entail. As such, there are very few publications that address the exceptional position of this project in the context of Le Corbusier's agenda for living and his body of work.

At the start of this study this notion of a designed project, an 'artistic' work, with its inherent intentions and distinctive language is something that, as an architect, shaped both my early expectations and critique of the project. Over the four year duration of this research our viewpoint and the basis of critique developed. This new position has affected the way we look at the success of architecture in the context of housing.

The text will briefly address the Unité project, its parameters, and the contexts of Briey, before moving to discuss Pessac as an important prototype; both for Le Corbusier and as a social housing comparator to further evaluate the Briey Unité. From then to the more recent present we introduce a relevant situation with Jean Nouvel's social housing project at Nimes, leading to notions of how we evaluate 'success' in social housing design. In considering Briey today we present edited interview data from four different residents, addressing the nature and scope of adaptations they have applied to the Unité. We additionally incorporate interpretations of the Briey Unité, and a summary evaluation as a participating observer, and conclude with images of images of the project's construction.

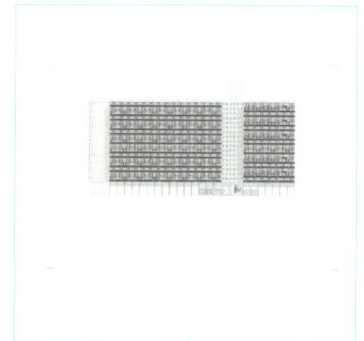

a

11

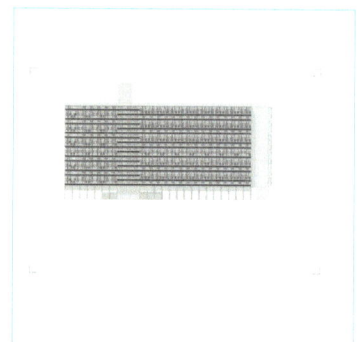

b

12

Drawings:

pages 11–12:
a. Drawing of the front elevation, 2018. The building differs from the other Unités due to the lack of an internal shopping street and social spaces: the flat roof, nursery and running track. This resulted in a plainer elevation consisting of only apartments.
b. Briey Únite's rear elevation.

The residents

Over a period between 2015 and 2018, we visited the Unité in Briey eight times to meet residents and interview them for this project. They have given a critical insight into their personal lives and the diversity of approaches they have applied towards inhabiting the building.

Each of the apartments visited is the primary residence of its owner(s), and has undergone significant transformations, with only a few original design items remaining in situ.

Distributed throughout this document you will encounter the interiors of four of the residents generous enough to share a real-life momentary record of their adaptations.

Beginning with Long term resident Pascal, the remaining three have been renamed as Ke1, Vi4 and Cl6 in respect of their privacy.

Resident: Pascal

19

a

a

b

c   d

Images:

e

f   g

pages 18–19:

a.   Briey in transition, 1989. In the 80s and 90s the Unité in Briey was partially abandoned. Schoening squatted the building with a group of architects in an effort to rescue it. The images are a document of the vandalised apartments that had been stripped of their Le Corbusier elements. Photographs by Pascal.

pages 20–23:

b.   Pascal at home in his living room.
c.   Front door.
d.   Adapted interior stair.
e.   Interior living spaces.
f.   Study area.
g.   Detail of Pascal's adaptations.

Pascal:

In a duplex on the Première Rue (as the lowest central corridor is called), with an entrance at the bottom level, no double-height space, lives Pascal Schoening; 79 years of age, architect, author and former educator. Pascal has been involved in the transformation of the Unité d'Habitation de Briey since 1989, before making Briey his official home in 2009.

Pascal was one of the first people to get involved in the rescue efforts of the Unité. He describes that when he arrived, the Première Rue was used as a dumping ground for all the rubble from the changes to the upper floors made by the Nursing school. With the help of like-minded people, they managed to clear the street and restore access. During his early years they squatted without paying rent which in turn attracted a series of fellow artists to the building.

Initially, his apartment was merely a shell with an original stair. Instead of attempting to restore the frameworks of the original interior, he opted for a more ingenious use of the found materials—mainly leftover original doors dug out from heaps of rubble and dead rats. A survey of his apartment revealed some 42 original doors adapted as panels and used to create living spaces and partition off areas—together with built-in furniture elements of the shop from the ground floor re-incorporated here as a low storage unit. One door became a new handrail for the stair, another two the balustrade, six doors form a partition to a downstairs guest room where a bed made out of yet another door blank resides. His own wardrobe—a VHS video cassette archive—consists of five further doors. A row of tables was constructed of 13 doors and his office uses a further three. The remainder are distributed throughout the apartment, propped up by clamps and pieces of wood. Pascal rescued the only original door to his apartment with its number '123' painted on it, which is now part of his bookshelf.

The original architectural interior layout was also significantly altered, with the kitchen now relocated to the centre of the upstairs cell. All of the fitting out, the built furniture, is of a temporary nature—being easily modified or removable in response to the changing needs of a resident.

Pascal, being an architect, has naturally a strong connection to the building. There is a constant stream of visitors and Pascal has amassed a lot of stories. He spends most of his time reading on his sofa, surrounded by the artefacts and collected fragments he has accumulated over the years.

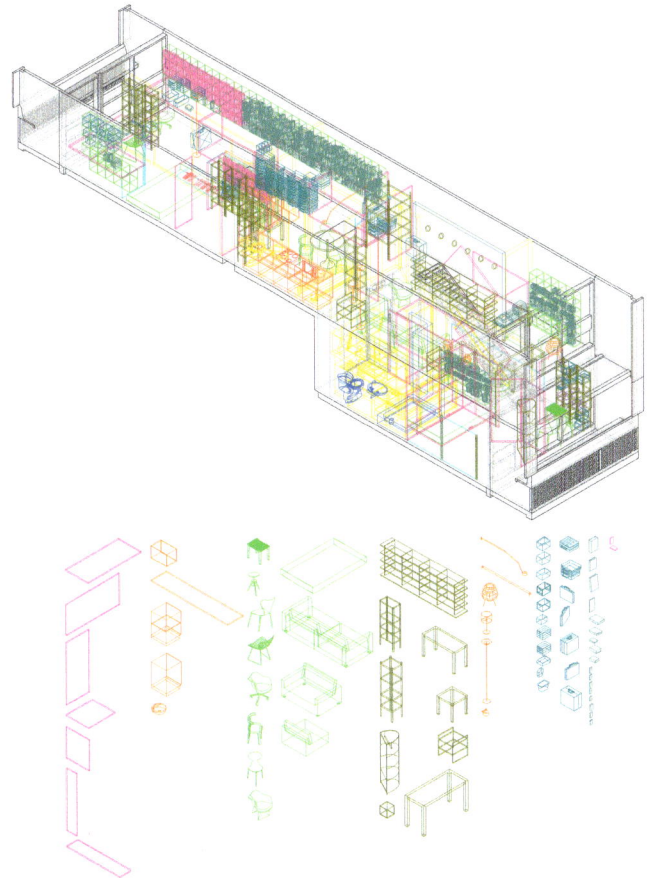

Drawing:

above: Taxonomy of elements in Pascal's apartment, 2017–18. The drawing explores the original lost building elements in yellow, alongside new additions, including furniture.

Le Corbusier: Unité d'Habitation,

Briey-en-Forêt, France

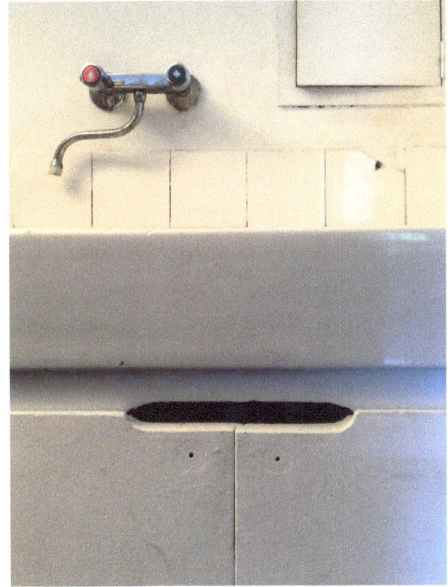

1950   **1960**   **1970**   **1980**

Restart of the Lorraine Steel Industry. Initiation of a municipal development plan.

"Satellite city" site chosen, 2km from the historic city center. The site was originally intended to host a range of different buildings, including a chopping center primary school nursery and church.

Soon after completion a new urban policy is announced that halts further development of the area, thereby isolating the Unite from the city.

1963: Regional economic crisis results in the local mining industry's first layoffs. Local population starts to decline.

1965: Le Corbusier dies. 1966: France withdraws from NATO.

Lorraine's regional economic crisis deepens.

From 1975 to 1982 the region is estimated to have lost 18000 people.

1983: After a vote by the General Council a process if decommissioning and demolition is decided. The last 121 families are to be relocated, of which 83 remain by summer.

The design development took place from the fall of '54 to '56

Work on site commences after 3 years of 'local political struggles and misunderstandings raised by the designs of Le Corbusier' in 1959

1961: Building is complete with 339 duplex apartments over 17 floors with six internal 'streets', and fully occupied by eight nationalities: the French (Algeria Métropole +) form two-thirds of the inhabitants, followed by the Italians (25%) and by a minority of Hungarian workers, Yugoslavian, Polish, Spanish, Irish and Swiss.

Brief respite for the Unite's declining population is found when a local US Army base 25km from Briey reserves 59 apartments of the Unite.

US forces leave as a consequence of Frances withdrawal, leaving the 59 apartments of Sixth Street empty. The building quickly becomes 30% vacant.

New work is undertaken: 'construction of the entrance of the building and its surroundings, adding a boiler and elevator, restoration waterproofing, creating a car park, restoration of dozens of apartments ... A breath of optimism then Briey-en-Forêt. The "denigration which has too long suffered the radiant city" seem to fade.'

Unite population was restored (1973–1975) after the new works.

Unite population unfortunately declines as the number of empty units rises from 50 in 1977 to 145 in 1980. Unite apartments are rented, and so many of the residents leave to buy nearby housing recently renovated by the private sector.

1980: Le Monde article states that: Briey is covered in graffiti, garbage chutes bearing black trickles, sticking filthy mailboxes are gutted, the plaster and tiles are flaked. Plastic ground dozens missing (?).

By 1982: 200 units are empty. In March '82 the union of tenents makes contact with the school of Architecture at Nancy. By October a workshop is established to explore the feasibility of saving the building.

1983: over the spring and summer 20 projects from the workshop are exhibited where Andre Wogensecky (a long standing collaborator of Le Corbusier) delivers a lecture that helps inspire the remaining 83 families to launch a preservation committee. By 1984 however, the building is empty.

Marseille Unité completes (1945–52)

Nantes-Rezé Unité completes (1948–55)

Berlin Unité completes (1956–58)

Briey Unité completes (1958–61)

Firminy Unité completes (1965–67)

1990   **2000**   **2010**   **2020**

1985: Guy Vattier, a newly elected Mayor commits to finding a way to save the building. A plan is eventually derived to sell part of the building to a nearby nursing school, as an alternative to a new building.

March–April 1987 after delays this proposal is rejected by the hospital. Guy Vattier organises a press conference where administrative innefficiencies are exposed. One day later a minister permits the immediate sale of the whole building to the hospital for 1 Franc. May: a mob violently loots and strips out 150 apartments. Summer: rennovation of the upper floors is undertaken by the hospital.

After the construction of the nursing school (including four function apartments, 48 studios, redistribution of partition walls, repainting of concrete walls and the installation of a new Boiler on the roof), the hospital sells the remaining two-thirds of the building to a private developer to rennovate the housing (including new lifts and the joining of some apartments) and public areas.

After 3 years of sales all units are sold by March 1991. Excluding the 'first street's 34 apartments reserved for the association of architects and artists with the aim of creating a "European center architecture research" insigated by the Mayor.

1993: The facade, columns, 'first street' and seven units are listed as historical monuments for protection, and a model apartment is established.

2003: An exhibition "Chronicles of a vertical village" traces the inhabitants of the building, helping to shape the reputation of the "First street' as an organisation.

2010: Briey Apartment staircase, built by Jean Prouvé Studio, sold at auction for $22250

2018: The last 'empty' apartment was sold.

31

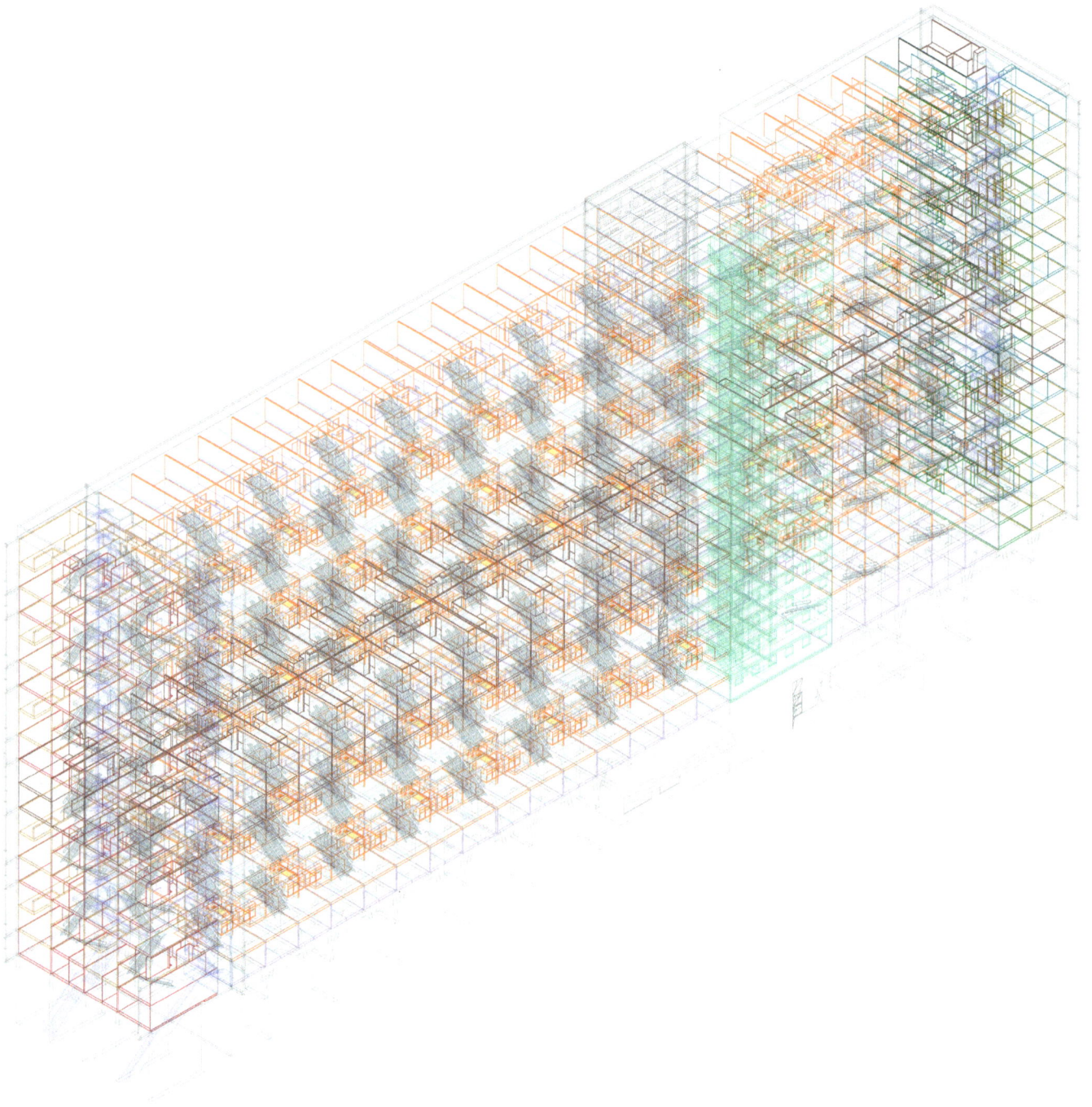

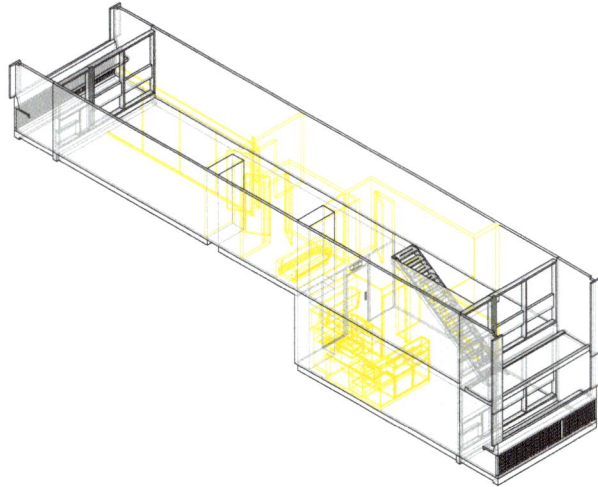
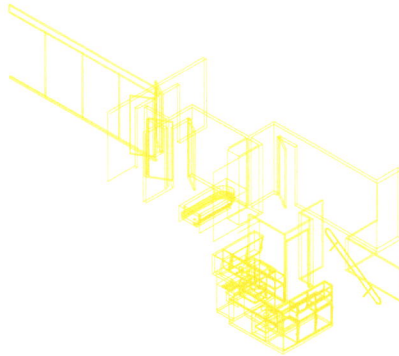

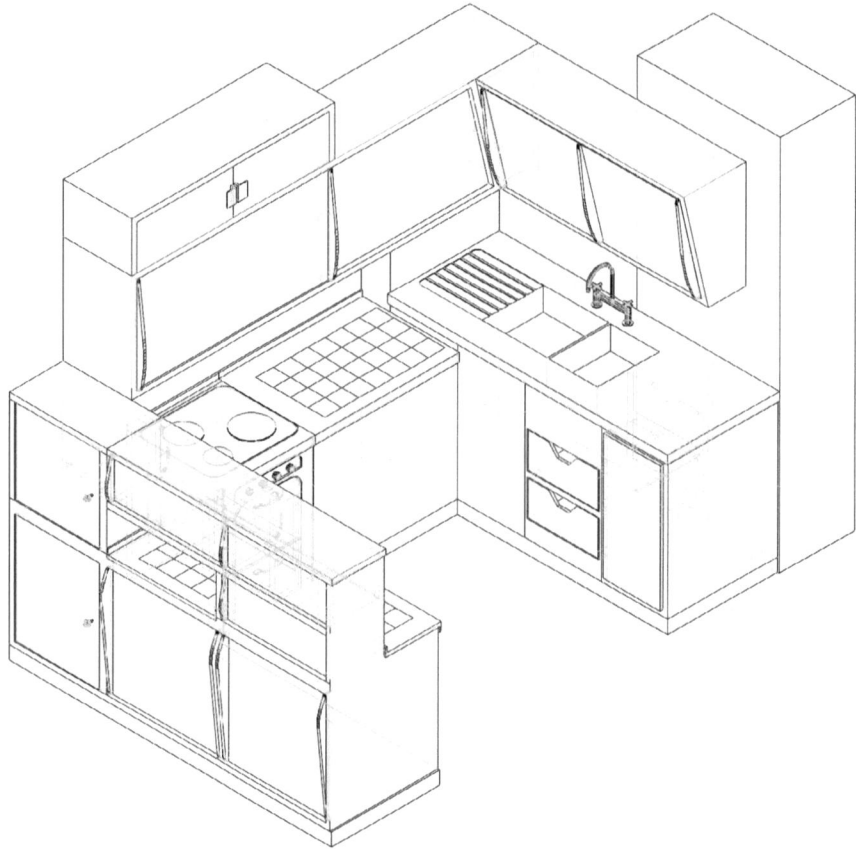

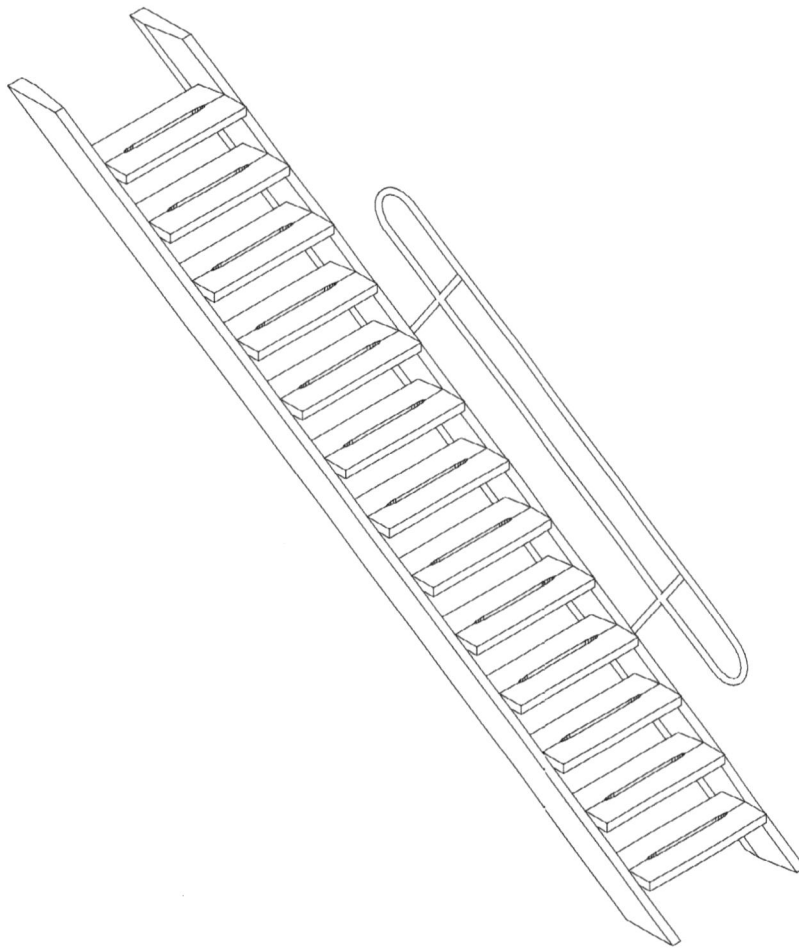

a

a

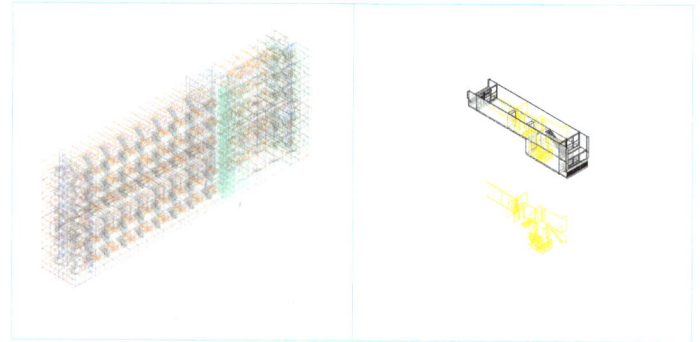

c

d

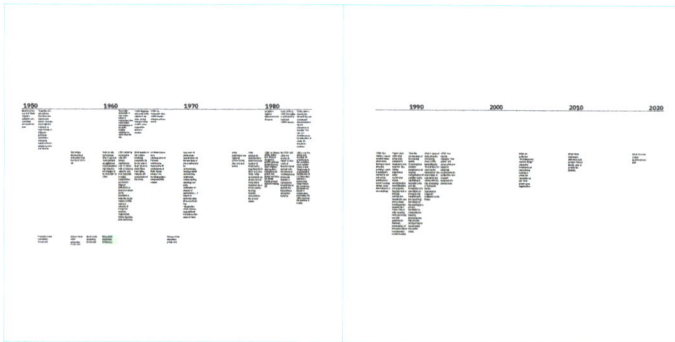

b

b

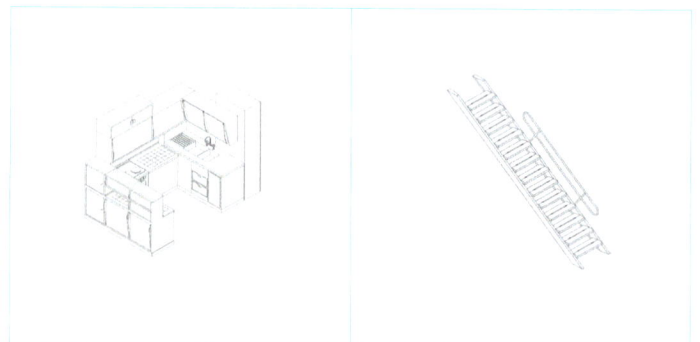

e

f

Images:

pages 28–29:
a. Photographs of the restored heritage apartment.

pages 30–35:
b. A timeline of the Briey Unité.
c. The Unité as intended, depicted as an isonometric study, 2019. This drawing outlines the original layout of the apartments and the built-in furniture fittings as part of Le Corbusier's 'ideal' arrangement.
d. Apartment drawings, 2017–18. This drawing of a typical apartment explores the original lost building elements, as indicated in yellow.
e. Drawing of a typical original kitchen, as designed by Charlotte Perriande.
f. Drawing of a typical original interior stair, as designed by Jean Prouvé.

Le Corbusier: Unité d'Habitation, Briey-en-Forêt, France

The Unité in Briey in the Lorraine area close to the border of Luxembourg, was built as part of the HLM (Habitation à Loyer Modéré or "rent-controlled housing"). As such, the building lacked many of the features we as architects associate with the Unité's: The nursery and the swimming pool on the roof was never completed due to budget restrictions and due to the fact that it was considered a folly idea. A conventional building housing a nursery was built instead close to the Unité. There is no internal shopping street, no shops were realised at all within the building. A Co-op was set up during the construction of the building but it closed as soon as it was completed. From the start, being located on top of the hill with no real public transport links and, due to the times, very little private car ownership the situation was far from optimal.

The ideal Unité format was inspired by the compact self-sustaining composition of the cruise ship and was designed in accordance with Le Corbusier's principles of the house as 'a machine for living in', an expression from his 1927 manifesto Vers Une Architecture (Towards A New Architecture), which described how modern dwellings—and to an extent the city—should operate. Based on a largely self-contained mixed programme, the Unité aimed to incorporate many of the diverse services one might associate with a functioning town: a nursery, shops, restaurants, community spaces, a hotel and a laundry.

Designed with 339 duplex apartment units for approximately 800 inhabitants over 17 floors and six internal 'streets', the Unité at Briey stands as the only Le Corbusier building built under the Habitation à loyer modéré (HLM) rent-controlled housing scheme in France. It was not, however, realised to the same construction standards or mixed programme of occupation as its four more valued siblings, and from the outset, this Unité—also known as Cité Radieuse (Radiant City)—was compromised.

Very soon after completion in 1961, the steady decline of the steel industry and therefore the mining industry in France impacted the closure of Briey's iron ore mines, a significant driver of the local economy. Eventually, as a consequence of the recession the building became less than half occupied. This in turn created a problem for the remaining residents who felt abandoned and isolated on top of the hill above the town. By 1979 it was partially squatted by a local homeless population, eventually the building fabric became more and more neglected with much of its fitted interior furnishings having been stripped out, sold or consumed as firewood. As such, by 1983 a demolition order was given to finally solve this problem. But in 1984 a new mayor, Guy Vattier, refused the demolition order, sold part of the building to the local hospital to install a nursing school—extensively remodelling part of an upper floor—and sold the remainder to a developer. With the help of Ron Howard, an architect and educator from the University of East London, they managed to change the public perception of the building. In 1993 after a long process of negotiation the exterior of the building was listed as a 'Monument Historiques', but a majority was left to the inhabitants to adapt to their personal needs. Within this remainder, the unit arrangement has itself been altered, with some units combined and some entrances changed, further reducing the total number of individual apartments.

J Abram and G Vattier's 'Le Corbusier à Briey' (2006)[1], co-written by the former town mayor who was instrumental in the recovery of the building, is currently one of the only published texts specifically addressing the history of this Unité, surrounding political turmoil and near demolition. This text takes a non-critical position and reflects one of the very few comprehensive studies of this Unités story, reframed and summarised in the timeline diagram of page 21–22. Given the nature of their title, and (importantly) the interests and pivotal role played by Guy Vattier in saving the building, the framing of the subject addresses the idea of the project as a 'Le Corbusier'. As such, in the recounting of the project's history and context this layer of the Unité's narrative has a greater presence than, for example, evaluations of the quality of the project as housing.

1.   Abram, J. and Vattier, G. (2006). Le Corbusier à Briey. Paris: Place.

Resident: Ke1

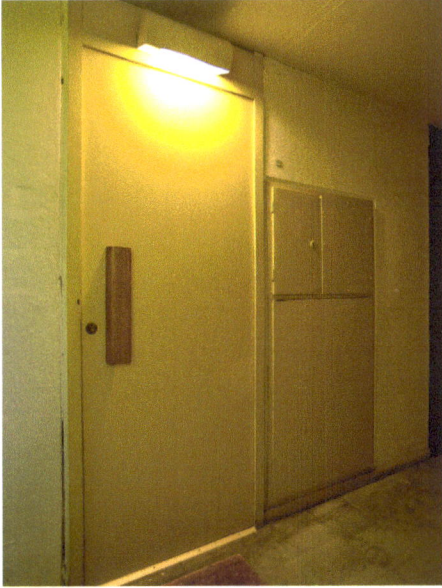

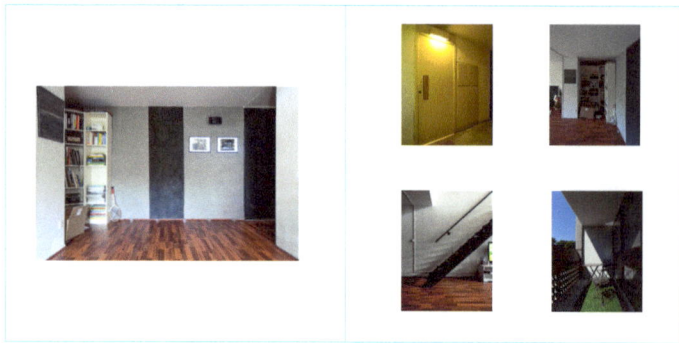

a
b
c
a
d

Images:

pages 40–41:
a. Entrance circulation space.
b. Front door as typical entrance from Unité internal street.
c. Adapted Jean Prouvé stair.
d. Balcony view.

Resident Ke1:

Première Rue duplex, entrance at the upper level, no double height space. 37 years of age, works in a bank, single, his first apartment, a keen art lover.

Ke1 has always been interested in art and is a regular visitor to galleries in Metz and London. But the main reason he chose to live in the Unité in Briey was the cost of the apartment. Being his first home he has a limited budget available for renovation.

Ke1 bought an apartment on the Première Rue. He can still remember the place from his youth when he attended illegal parties in the empty apartments.

When he moved in there was nothing there with most of the interior fittings being broken or unsalvageable with the stair being the only original feature worth saving. He occupies an end apartment that was set up for a family with two children. In the process of adapting the space Ke1 removed all interior partitions to open up the floorplan. A new kitchen was designed by a kitchen company, the steel handrail for the stairs by a friend working in a nearby metal factory. Facing one of the emergency escape stairs Ke1 covered one of the back walls with faux concrete on Styrofoam panelling. Although it is located on the lowest level of the building the apartment has no insulation to the open space of the ground floor. As a remedy, a new laminate flooring with a thin layer of insulation was installed to the completed space.

His favourite area is the new kitchen where he can sit and entertain friends. He likes that his apartment feels modern, the scented candles and faux grass on the balcony make the space feel like home.

Contexts of Briey

Observational reflections:

From the outset, the notion of a designed project—an 'artistic' work—with its inherent intentions and distinctive language is something that shaped both early expectations and a personal critique of the project. Over the four years of research, a new viewpoint and critical position emerged, questioning the idea of 'success' in architecture—specifically in housing—and how it might be assessed.

On visiting Briey, the atmosphere of the building's environs is inseparable from the rationality of its architecture. All early experiences of Briey as a project were instinctively and unfavourably compared with previous experiences of Le Corbusier projects world-wide. Additionally, as much of the fitted furniture had been removed, it was apparent across both public and private areas, the responsibilities of conveying the author's intentions were left to the concrete structure of the building.

In accordance with Le Corbusier's vision, the Unité d'Habitation was conceived as a machine for living and the buildings designed using the latest technologies and interpretations of social housing available. The rigid format of inhabitation embedded in its apartment typologies and the built-in furniture—a reflection of the times in which it was installed—was, however, unable to reflect surrounding social and technological changes.

As most of the original interiors were lost over the years, either used as firewood for a homeless population or sold on international auction sites as original Le Corbusier fittings, much of the conservation efforts were reduced to the Première Rue. Yet almost all elements signifying Le Corbusier's designs—the doors and the wooden door handles, ironmongery, the lights above the doors, and the 'original' colour scheme of the corridors is now an approximation, leaving the interior experience with a sense of pastiche. The interior transformations were extensive, including the kitchens which, although designed by Charlotte Perriand, were almost universally too small for contemporary use, replaced instead with contemporary solutions sourced from the local DIY store Mr. Bricolage. Echoing sentiments and interpretations of Pessac, I imagined and believed that Le Corbusier would not have been happy with the outcome of this project.

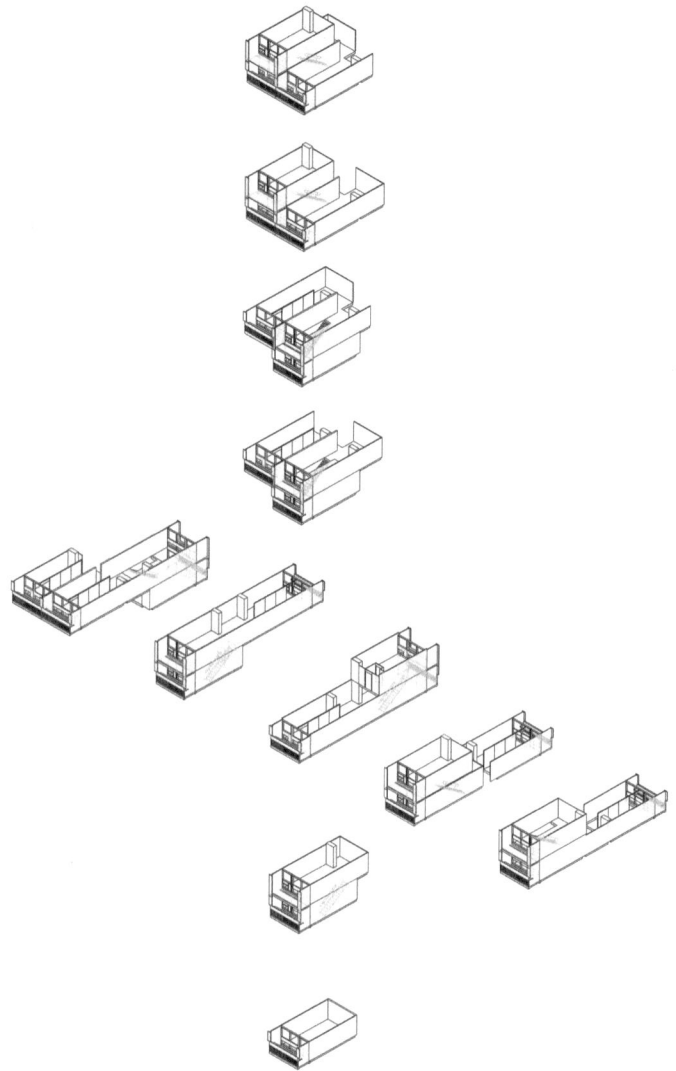

Drawing:

above: Unité apartment unit configurations.

Contexts of Briey

From the outset, the situation of this Unité also known as the Cité Radieuse (Radiant City) was compromised. André Wogenscky (a long standing collaborator of Le Corbusier's) said in 1983 about the context of the housing Unité at Briey, *"The fit was not good, neither geographically nor economically, or sociologically."* [2] Ordinarily, in hindsight there may be an escape in accusing the context of failing a project. However, in the case of this Unité, there are four further comparable and arguably more recognised iterations of essentially the same form and intention in differing contexts. In this regard, in a simplistic comparative study, the most and least widely acknowledged of these could be taken as reference data.

The five built Unité projects are, in order of their construction:

- Unité d'Habitation of Marseille in 1952,
- Unité d'Habitation of Nantes-Rezé in 1955,
- Unité d'Habitation of Berlin Westend in 1957,
- **Unité d'Habitation of Briey-en-Forêt in 1961,**
- Unité d'Habitation of Firminy-Vert in 1965.

All Unité's take the same archetypal form of a multi-storey slab block oriented so the apartments face in an East-West direction. Although the exterior is dominated by the appearance of a uniform grid the interior organisation house interlocking alternating combinations of single storey, dual aspect, and double height apartment units, with interiors featuring stairs designed by Jean Prouvé, and kitchen designed by Charlotte Perriand—as so for the other Unité's. Beyond form, the Unité principle, derived from Le Corbusier's earlier proposed utopian urbanism projects, came to represent a new housing typology whilst borrowing principles of organisation and self sufficiency from the Ocean liner.[3] In the Unité, the singular architectural form is enriched with the services and facilities imagined of a well functioning modern city. This was the culmination of a slow development, the theoretical basis of which dated back to Le Corbusier's early propositions for a utopian urbanism, aspirational plans for the 'vertical garden city' (cité-jardin verticale) dated back to the 1920's and were indirectly influenced by Ebenezer Howard's Letchworth Garden City and his book 'Garden Cities of Tomorrow'. But for Le Corbusier the figure-ground relationship of the Garden City would be further polarised into a continuous landscape touched lightly by high density urbanised forms, garden ground plus housed-cities. The high density *Ville contemporaine de trois millions d'habitants* an unlocated city for 3 million inhabitants, he designed with Pierre Jeanneret in 1922 and published in Oeuvre complète, volume-1 [4] was a key step in the formalisation of this agenda. As a building format, it was further inspired by his observations of the Soviet communal housing project, in particular, the Narkomfin Building in Moscow (1932)—designed by Moisei Ginzburg—as precedent study.

Of the Unités the original Marseille project is considered in many ways as a prototype. The diverse internal programme includes shops, educational facilities (including a children's art school), a publicly accessible hotel, and a restaurant. In keeping with the concept of a stacked urbanism, these services are organised around interim floors designated as 'streets'. The flat roof, designated as aerial landscape, is designed as a communal terrace incorporating a shallow paddling pool for children, space for theatrical performances, a gallery, and a running track.

With some variation this programmatic make-up was repeated as an integral part of the ensuing Unité's—with the notable exception of Briey where, owing to budgets, politics, and in some part its designation as social housing, the programme mix was significantly compromised and the scope of the project reduced.

Thus, to return to Wogenscky's critique of the Briey Unité's context, a more balanced assessment should factor in the wider realisation of the Unité project—comparing not just the Briey context with other Unité contexts, but the Briey Unité and its diminished inner programme with other more complete Unité's.

2. Abram, J. and Vattier, G. (2006). Le Corbusier à Briey. Paris: Place. pp.74.
3. "The Steamship Is The First Stage In The Realization Of A World Organized According To The New Spirit." Le Corbusier.
4. Le Corbusier and Pierre Jeanneret, Oeuvre complète, volume-1, 1910-1929.

Resident: Vi4

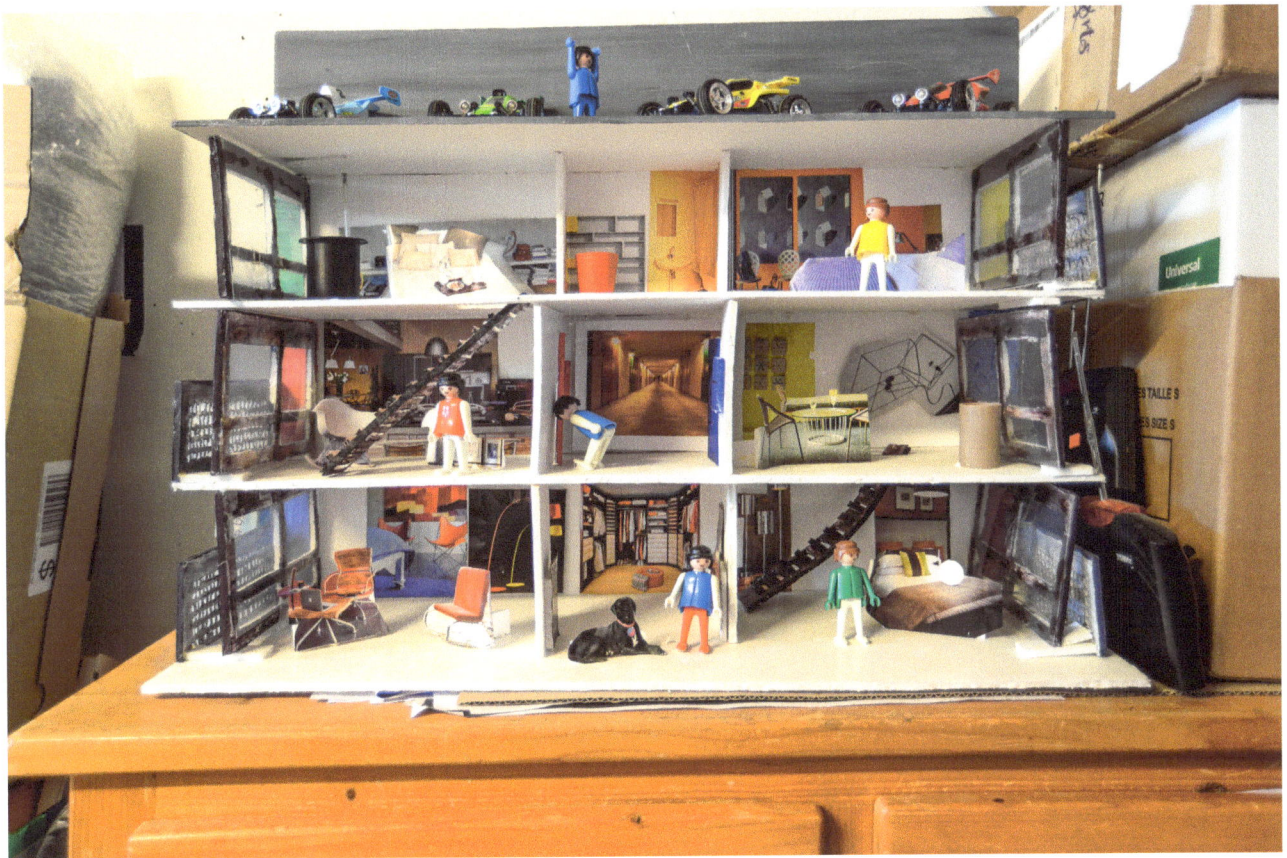

a

b

c

c

Images:

pages 50–51:
a. Original Jean Prouvé stair.
b. Interior.

pages 52–53:
c. Youth Club appropriation.

Resident Vi4:

4th Rue duplex at the end of the building, entrance at the lower level, no double height space. 39 years of age, lives with his wife, three children and a dog, head of the Unité residents association.

Vi4 has headed the residents association for two years and knows the majority of the other Unité residents. After moving in in 1991, he purchased his apartment ten years later. He loves the patchwork the community represents. Looking back he says he was 'insane to move in but it was cheap and the place was enormous'.

His apartment has two units at the bottom and four at the top level including three bathrooms. Apart from the stair there are no remaining original features. He has extensively updated his apartment over the years since moving in, including panelling the ceiling and creating a bigger kitchen at the lower level. This new kitchen area has a central unit and echoes the original kitchen arrangement—originally designed not by Le Corbusier but by Charlotte Perriand (1903–1999), a fellow architect and collaborator. All the work was carried out by himself, though lately they are thinking of re-exposing the original ceiling as per other apartments.

Vi4 has recently divided his DJ studio to make space for another bedroom for his baby daughter. In order to visualise the space he has planned the partition on a free and open source 3D gaming software called Blender. He sourced the materials from the local DIY store and built the partition with Melamine chipboard.

For Vi4 the whole of the building is his home, he regularly organises a youth club which makes use of one of the empty apartments and, for the younger children, organises treasure-hunts that make use of the whole building.

Pessac and Nemes

a

b

c

d

Modern Quarter Fruges (Q.M.F), Pessac, France

From the remoteness of the Unité's location and proposed communal facilities we see an intent for a focussed community, to the size and nature of the interior kitchen designs as a reflection of social ritual, here for example we might see an intention for the greater use of communal restaurants than private dining. Further consideration is needed to distinguish between an Architect's intentions and prevailing attitudes of the time.

These considerations are present in both his text and his works. In this instance we see his attitudes to various notions, from thermal comfort, to movement, to his notions of community. To a greater extent his intentions are also present in his experience of the Pessac project resident alterations as detailed by Boudon's 1979 study; Lived-in Architecture: Le Corbusier's Pessac Revisited.

Commissioned in 1920 by Henry Frugès, a wealthy eccentric Sugar magnate, and realised just over half a decade later almost 40 years prior to Briey, the workers' accommodation complex of 50 (intended to be 135) modernist houses designed by Le Corbusier represented the actualization of an experiment on a plot in the Le Monteil district of Pessac near the city of Bordeaux.

Henry Frugès, whose aims were socially oriented, intended the units for all levels of his staff and their families, and urged Le Corbusier to exercise the full extent of his theories:

"I authorise you to put your theories into practice, however extreme the consequences might be. I would like to achieve conclusive results in a new form of inexpensive living quarters. Pessac must be a laboratory. I authorise you to break with all conventions and abandon traditional methods." [5]

Additionally, as an experiment, Pessac was very much concerned with town-planning (to bring together and support the community), and exploring standardisation in construction (to save on cost). The brightly painted Béton Brut minimal outcome is still said to feel contemporary by today's standards. However, at the time, given its hard edges and austere surfaces it was seen to be unlike anything else of the time and in conflict with nearby Bordeaux's mixture of post-renaissance classical styles. Despite its modern facilities: heating, running water, and septic tanks many of the workers felt it was too avant-garde and refused to move in. Shortly after, with a backdrop of negative criticism from Bordeaux's architects and Frugès own financial decline (and subsequent depression), the predominantly vacant project was sold at a loss to a private developer. Eventually the new tenants made several forms of modifications to their homes in response to their own sensibilities and needs: some superficial, some spatial—introducing extensions, new openings, new divisions. When Le Corbusier saw the changes, he was heard to have said:

'Connaissez-vous, c'est toujours la vie qui a raison, l'architecte qui a tort.' / 'You know, it's always life that is right and the architect who is wrong.' [6]

As a reference project, Pessac already touches on many of this study's initial questions, however, Le Corbusier's reflection here reiterates and raises further questions regarding his experience and attitude towards inhabitation on embarking on the Unités, and in particular Briey—given the similarities in their socialist agendas and target demographic. [7]

5. Excerpt from: 'Le Corbusier et Jeanneret deux confrères 1910–1929'(Zurich).
6. Boudon, P. (1979). Lived-in architecture. Cambridge, Mass: MIT Press, pp. 1, 65.
7. A Post Occupancy Evaluation was documented in greater depth in Phillipe Boudon's 'Lived-in Architecture: Le Corbusier's Pessac Revisited' (further discussed in Fred Scott's 'On Altering Architecture') and reassessed in Ada Louise Huxtable's 1986 essay 'Architecture, anyone?: Reappraisal at Pessac' which builds upon Boudon's 1979 study by questioning previous critiques of the project's success (potential misinterpretations of Boudon's study), thus presenting an alternative interpretation of the resident's adaptations and resilience of Le Corbusier's intent.

a. Quartiers Modernes Frugès, Nov 2016.
b. Quartiers Modernes Frugès, Nov 2016.
c. Le Corbusier in 1964. Born: Charles-Édouard Jeanneret-Gris.
d. The Cité Frugès in Pessac on opening day. 1926, only 50 of the intended 153 units were completed. Corbusier's experimental building construction techniques were distrusted by local builders, and for three years the plumbers refused to integrate the project with the local water network.

a

b

Jean Nouvel: Nemausus, Nimes, France

A contemporary project that echoes many of the parameters of the Briey Unité can be found in Jean Nouvel's Nemausus 1 housing project in Nimes, France; researched and documented in the 1995 film Nemausus 1—A housing project of the 80s directed by Richard Copans and Stan Neumann.

When Jean Nouvel built the Nemausus social housing complex under HLM rules in Nimes, France, in 1987, he fought with the developer to be more generous with the volumes of the individual apartments and negotiated a trade-off for delivering a 30% cheaper building in exchange for 30% larger apartments. However, as rents were in proportion to floor area, this later presented something of a paradox for the idea of generous social housing and, as such, this prototype was never repeated.

The individual units feature a double-height space, an open-plan arrangement, and open spaces at both front and back—even on the upper floors. At first sight, the building must have appeared to be a desirable place to live. But in actuality, each tenant was obliged to sign a tenancy agreement preventing them from decorating their apartments, thus retaining the space and the structure as Nouvel intended— bare concrete walls, exposed services, even 'fake' builders' markings, plumb lines and fitting instructions on the walls. Eventually the tenants rebelled against this rule, viewing it as an imposition, by engaging with the fabric of the building and tight restrictions—walls were covered in wallpaper and paint, floors with carpets, curtains were used to screen off private areas, cornices blurred the lines between the walls and the ceilings. The spaces were personalised and adapted to reflect the inhabitant's sense of taste and understanding of comfort. [8]

Nouvel frames the agreement and subsequent rejection as a mechanism; enabling him to see the difference between how people say they will live, and how people want to live. If we expand on this notion, does the agreement, the instance of a resident's arrival, mark a transition from a building design stage to an interior design stage?

Does the first stage need to be fully designed (decisions made and asserted) to enable the second stage to take place? Would it be possible to recognise social (or other) housing of this nature as developing over a two-stage design process?

8. Nemausus 1 - A housing project of the 80's. (1995). [DVD] Directed by R. Copans and S. Neumann. France: Illuminations Media.

a. Jean Nouvel - Nemausus Apartments, Nimes, 1987-94.
b. Jean Nouvel presenting his projects at Odeon, Vienna, September 2009.

Resident: Cl6

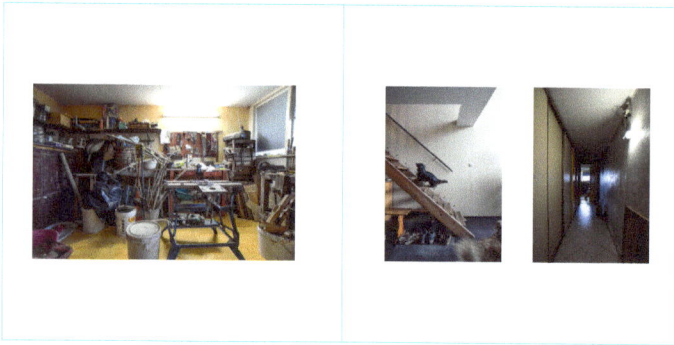

a

64   65

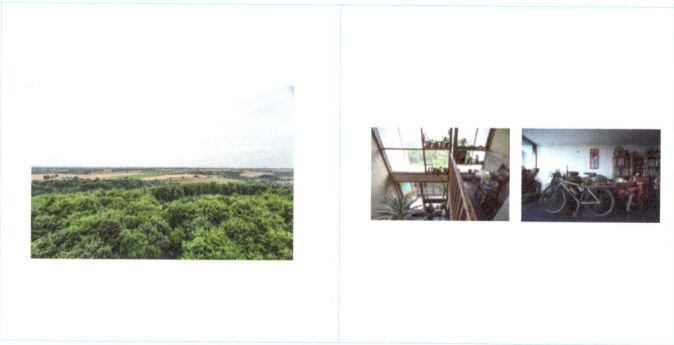

d

66   67

Images:

pages 64–67:
a. Converted workshop space.
b. Adapted Jean Prouvé stair.
c. Cl6's interior.
d. View from within.
e. Mezzanine and interior.

Resident Cl6:

6th Rue duplex, entrance at the bottom level, double height space. The gardener lives in the apartment with his wife and a dog and uses it as a workshop.

Of all the residents, Cl6's apartment is the most surprising. He works as a gardener and loves to build treehouses. He keeps most of his work tools in his apartment. The downstairs entrance area is occupied by chainsaws, a strimmer and beekeeping equipment. An aroma of honey draws you to the honey centrifuge positioned in the corner, the rest of the space is furnished with self-made furniture, and made homely by a variety of plants.

The upstairs is like a Wunderkammer; you never know what is around the next corner. Like many of the other apartments the stair is the only surviving element from the original fit-out. Cl6 has transformed the space though colour and an eclectic mix of furniture. The space behind the sofa is used as a botanical nursery for plant seedlings, and he has set up a full woodworking workshop in one of the former bedrooms. Here he realises his projects: wooden benches, chairs, and turned candlesticks that can be found all around the apartment. Recently he has become more interested in the building. Walls have been stripped back to the raw concrete and he has started to experiment with primary colours emulating those used in the renovation of the corridors.

Cl6 is very proud of the space he has created for his wife. He likes the connection of the plants on the inside with the views into the surrounding countryside.

Four residents: in conclusion

Where many of Le Corbusier's ideals were based on principles—proportions, societal ideals, construction strategies and urban design approaches, to name but a few—the Unités have withstood, accommodated, and reflected the needs and intentions of others. Sometimes these intentions have focused on preservation while at other times accommodation. The results have on occasion become multi-dimensional and here at Briey it is felt that they warrant a varied approach in engaging with the project as it is today.

Examining the response data we see that this number reflects too small fraction of the Unité's total population in its 339 apartments to be considered representative. Furthermore, in assessing the participants' demographic distribution, we see that they are all relatively educated, physically able, male, adults. As such, to extrapolate, it could be that those who responded represented the most confident and adaptive (DIY active, building adaptive) residents, implying the remaining resident interiors may or may not have been equally modified. To better address this question further study would be required, plus ideally an interview with the one longest serving resident able to provide a complete oral history of the building and his experience. However, time and information provided by these four is still considered as valuable information and very useful in contributing to our own reflections on the nature of the building, and evaluations of the project's success.

Regarding the notion of adaptation and Le Corbusier's principles, it may help to consider the potential for reciprocity; it can happen both ways. An inhabitant may adapt a given architectural context, they may adapt themselves to that context, or perhaps more intrinsically some balance of the two.

By way of comparative reflection, the following quote from a QMF Pessac resident was recorded by Boudon as part of his study:

M8- 'That chimney... it is both well sited and badly sited... a chimney in the middle of a room, I find that disturbing and yet it is well sited because... because it not only provides a chimney, it also provides a corridor ...and, you know, you get used to it... and when you're used to it, you don't look at it in the same way... at first it was rather disturbing: I mean, a staircase in the middle of a room, it's odd... and the kitchen is also badly site because it's opposite a hall so you can't see anything it's good and bad, it's disturbing ... there are some things which don't seem to be in the right place... and yet they ... they are there. That's what's... that's what's good, precisely that!... but the staircase, now I find that is in the right place, because like that, flanking the dining-room, it has the effect of separating the two rooms without having a wall, it's good ... and it's not good at one and the same time...and that's what's good about it.' [9]

9.   Boudon, P. (1979). Lived-in architecture. Cambridge, Mass: MIT Press, pp.45.

The Streets /

Notions of Success

72

73

74

75

Images:

pages 72–75:
–.   Moments of circulation, the Unité's various internal streets.

Notions of success

Le Corbusier's Pessac and Nouvel's Nimes both touch upon key aspects of each of the earlier questions; the relationship between the artist-artwork-owner, architect-building-occupant, and the rights one has to determine or intervene in the actions of the other. The act of designing and the act of living exhibit consequences for the same shared materials, but in recognising these as two distinct 'acts' we separate the role of the architect, or the intention of the architect as author, and the role of the inhabitants in the act of dwelling. This latter role alludes to a subject discussed at length by many since Heidegger's seminal essay 'Building, Dwelling Thinking' [10] where, if 'building' can be understood as a form of 'dwelling' (in the sense of home and not merely being in a place), then it should follow that dwellers, the residents of Briey, may exhibit intentions to 'build' as an intrinsic aspect of their 'dwelling'—something Heideger views as speaking to our being in the world. In this way, could we view the documented expressions of the residents' adaptations as no more or less significant than those of Le Corbusier's? There is in addition a social, if not written, contract, that defines the status of the designed output (the already built) as a part of the world, to be dwelled within. As Bourdon observes:

' "All you have to do is ask the people who live in our villas how they feel about them and what it feels like to be living in them." -quote from the housing prospectus.

What a person feels about a house and what it feels like to be living in a house are two different things, the second of which, at least, can only be assessed by the occupant. In a manner of speaking, therefore, a house leads a dual existence on the one hand it is an object of intellectual and aesthetic analysis whilst on the other hand it is a container in which people live their lives.' [11]

Though we have seen with Nouvel's Nimes residents that there are boundaries between building and dwelling (or within contracts), these may be moved to suit the side with the greater will. Thus, if we consider the state of 'home' to be the final design achievement, then would it not be more appropriate to imagine 'adaptation' as the second half of a two stage design process? With the architectural design reflecting the outcome of the first? In the case of the QMF at Pessac it could be seen distance between building and dwelling measured over time, where the prescription of Le Corbusier's modernism was difficult for many at first, yet over time (a boundary) it attracted those willing to adapt it to their needs, and those willing to adapt to it. It is a testimony that, for all the residents alterations, the essence—or feeling—of Le Corbusier's design intentions and architectural aspiration is still noticeably present. As reflected by Huxtable on Pessac:

'The scale and relationship of the houses to one another and to the gardens are still strong and good. There is a feeling of a cohesive whole. Even with the loss of key elements of the "pure" Corbusian style ... Pessac retains an impressive and recognisable integrity. This is a very pleasant place to be. And the houses are clearly survivors.
It is also clear that Pessac is a survivor precisely because of its architecture. Its strong identity absorbs almost anything time and residents can inflict. Structurally the houses are incredibly solid. One can read the original features and then read the way they have been used or assimilated." [12]

In this manner, the author's intentions could be said to have survived, even if not to his complete satisfaction. Indeed, Fred Scott's On Altering Architecture[13] asks questions about the idea of authenticity in the light of restoration (a type of alteration) versus alteration itself in the absence of the author. It features a dialectical review of Pessac and Bourdan's work in noting the effects of the residents alterations he summarily observes that: 'The conflict was between the pure (Le Corbusier's position) and the colloquial (Local preferences).' He goes on to observe Boudan's study, in addressing the post completion alterations as it does, highlights the problematic relationship that architectural theory has with alteration:

'For Pessac to have remained unaltered, or to have appeared so, would have required that the populace behave as had Mme Schröder in her similarly sized and similarly aged house in Utrecht. One can imagine that such *discipline would be beyond any group of people, outside of the armed services or a religious order. However, this is the degree of rigour regarding the conduct of daily life that such day-to-day maintenance would require, year in, year out, regardless of the change of inhabitants ... . This in itself would contradict the liberation of daily life that the architect intended to promote through the design of these houses.'*

On closer inspection of Boudan's images of Pessac he reflects on the *'double nature'* of the *'vernacular'* and the *'magnificence of the original'*. Echoing Huxtable's sentiment, Scott notes that in sparing no regard for the author's original intentions, the vernacular alterations juxtapose with the structural proportions of the original work and thus permit the identities of each to coexist.

Given the relative similarities in circumstances, how many of these same reflections might be observed at Briey?

10. Heidegger, M., 1971. Building dwelling thinking, in Farrell Krell, D (ed.), Basic Writings: Martin Heidegger. London: Routledge, pp. 344-363.
11. Boudon, P. (1979). Lived-in architecture. Cambridge, Mass: MIT Press, pp.112.
12. Huxtable, A. (1986). Architecture, anyone?. New York: Random House, pp.17.
13. Scott, F. (2008). On altering architecture. London: Routledge. pp.24–34.

Under Construction

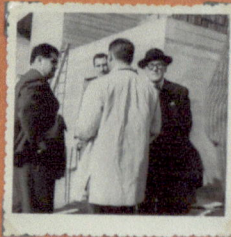

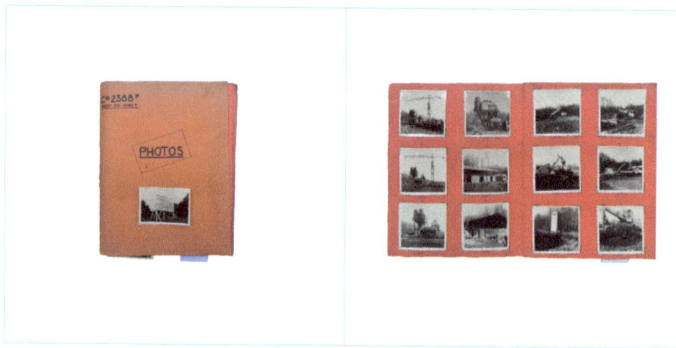

80

81

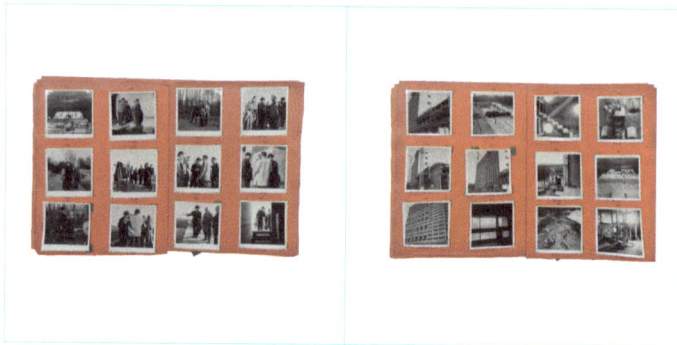

82

83

Images:

pages 80–83:

–. Photographs from the construction process, including photographs of Le Corbusier's inspection visit (p83 Black hat).

Bibliography / Images

Bibliography

◦ Abram, J. and G. Vattier (2006). Le Corbusier à Briey: Histoire mouvementée d'une Unité d'Habitation. Paris: Editions Jean-Michel Place.

◦ Boudon, P. (1979). Lived-In Architecture: Le Corbusier's Pessac Revisited. Cambridge, Mass: MIT Press.

◦ Copans, R. and S. Neumann. (1995) Nemausus 1 - A housing project of the 80s. France: Illuminations Media.

◦ Le Corbusier, C-E., W. Boesiger, P. Jeanneret and O. Stonorov. (1946) Le Corbusier and Pierre Jeanneret, Oeuvre complete de 1910-1929. Vol. 1. Zurich: Les Editions D'Architecture Erlenbach-Zurich.

◦ Le Corbusier, C-E. (1923) Vers une architecture. Paris: G. Crès.

◦ Heidegger, M. (1971) 'Building Dwelling Thinking'. Basic Writings: Martin Heidegger. London: Routledge.

◦ Howard, E. (1902) Garden Cities of To-morrow: Urban Planning. London: Swan Sonnenschein & Co.

◦ Huxtable, A. L. (1986) Architecture, Anyone? New York: Random House.

◦ Scott, F. (2008). On Altering Architecture. London: Routledge.

◦ Association La Première Rue. (2019) www.lapremiererue.fr/.

◦ Fondation Le Corbusier. (2019) www.fondationlecorbusier.fr/.

Image Credits

- p18, 19: Polaroid images ©Pascal Schoening, 1989.

- p58 a, b: Low-cost housing units built by Le Corbusier in the Cité Frugès in Pessac (1926). By JospBC, CC BY-SA 4.0. https://commons.wikimedia.org/wiki/File:Cit%C3%A9_Frug%C3%A8s,_Pessac_03.jpg#file

- p58 c: Le Corbusier (1964) Stedelijk Museum Sikkensprijzen. Joop van Bilsen / Anefo, CC0 1.0 Universal Public Domain Dedication. https://commons.wikimedia.org/wiki/File:Le_Corbusier_(1964).jpg

- p58 d: The Cité Frugès in Pessac on opening day. 1926. Public Domain

- p60 a: Jean Nouvel - Nemausus Apartments, Nimes, 1987-94. By Rory Hyde 2008, CC BY-SA 2.0. https://commons.wikimedia.org/wiki/File:Nemausus.jpg

- p60 b: Jean Nouvel presenting his projects at Odeon, Vienna, September 2009. By Christopher Ohmeyer 2009, CC BY-SA 2.0. https://commons.wikimedia.org/wiki/File:Jean_Nouvel_2009_Vienna_frontal.jpg.

- p80–83: Album photographs c/o the Briey Archive.

- All other photographs and drawings ©Patrick Weber.

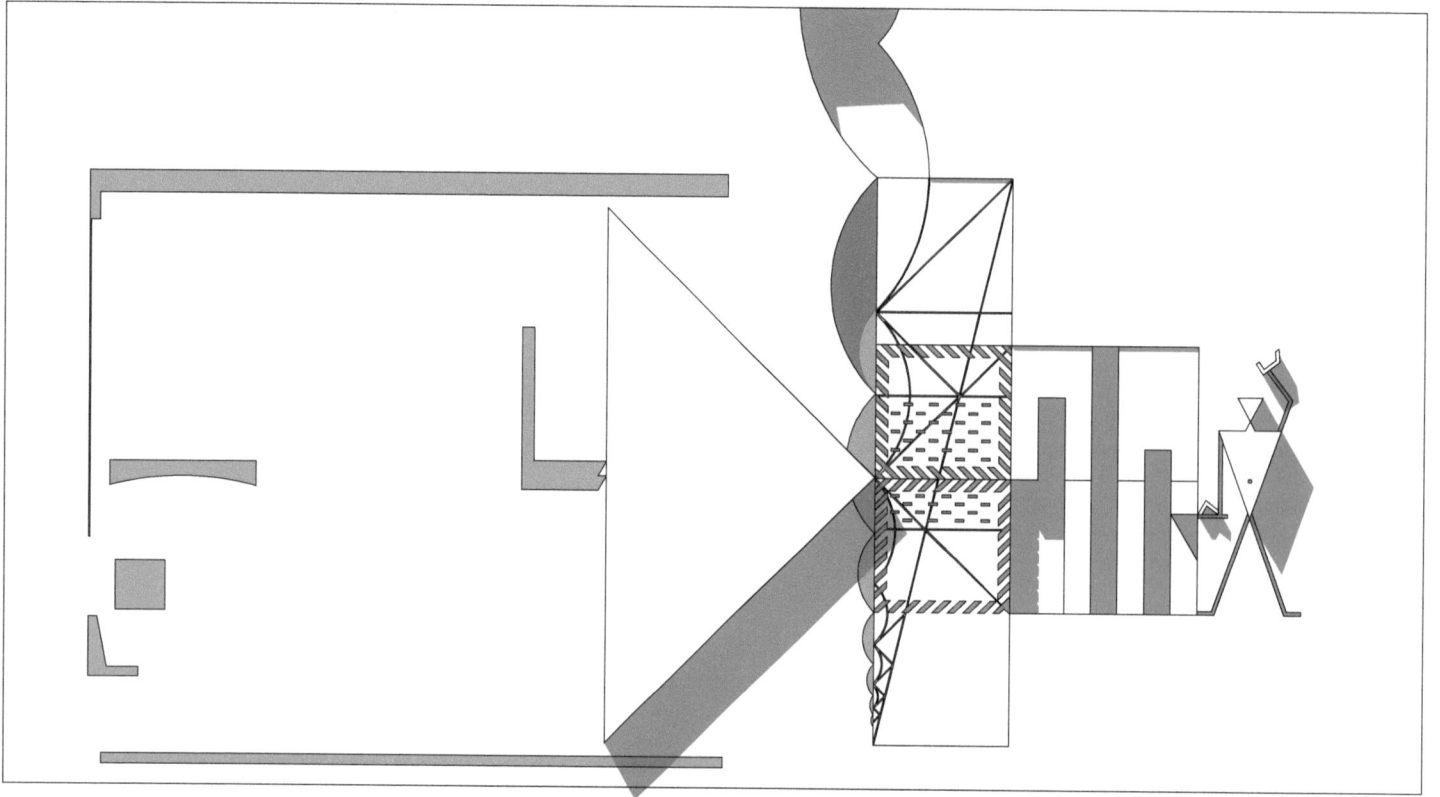